Mount Tremper has a Temper

By Thomas O'Grady

Illustrated by Karen Chapman

Published in 2022 by
Saratoga Springs Publishing, LLC
Saratoga Springs, NY 12866
Printed in the United States of America

ISBN-13: 978-1-955568-08-1
ISBN-10: 1-955568-08-1
Library of Congress Control Number:
2022909041
Text copyright © 2022 Thomas O'Grady
Illustrations copyright © 2022 Karen Chapman

Written by Thomas O'Grady
Illustrations by Karen Chapman
Graphic design by Karen Chapman
Publisher & book design by Vicki Addesso Dodd

Saratoga Springs Publishing's books are available
at a discount when purchased in quantity for
promotions, fundraising and educational use.
For additional information, book sales or events
contact us at www.SaratogaSpringsPublishing.com
or saratogaspringspublishing@gmail.com.

For my family, who shares in my adventures and inspires me to be the best version of myself. —TO

For my Dad, who kindled my love of art and design, and set me on a path of no return. —KC

Mount Tremper
has a temper.

And so would you.

Mount Tremper has a temper.

It's because Tremper is the smallest of the bunch.

4,000 FEET

MT TREMPER
2,740'
2,034' GAIN

3,000 FEET

2,000 FEET

MT REDHILL
2,990'
800' GAIN

1,000 FEET

SEA LEVEL

Mount Tremper
has a temper.

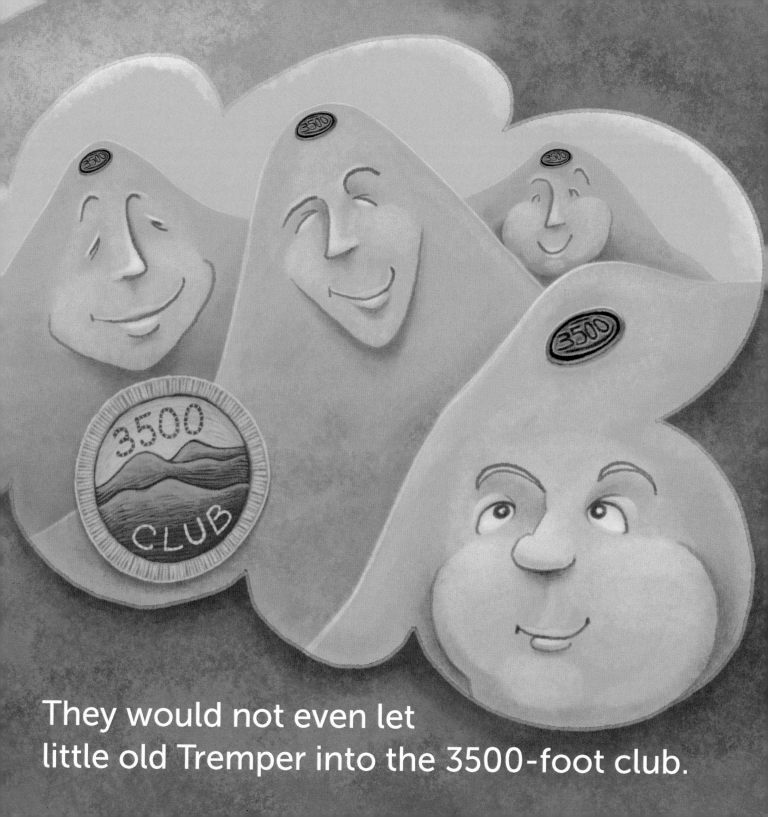

They would not even let
little old Tremper into the 3500-foot club.

Mount Tremper has a temper.

Tremper is
often overlooked.

Mount Tremper has a temper.

Tremper is not even one of the hundred highest mountains in the Catskills.

Wait a second!

Why should Mount Tremper have a temper when he has so much character to offer?

Look at all the beauty that gives Tremper his character!

Mount Tremper had a temper.

Tremper will make you climb
more than the rest.

And exercise is such a
great way to build your character.

Mount Tremper had a temper.

And did you know that Tremper has two lean-tos as well?

What an inviting place to spend the night should you decide to camp. Sharing is such a great way to build character!

Mount Tremper
had a temper.

Tremper also has his own rock quarry for you to explore.

But be careful! Rattlesnakes like rock quarries too, and they're part of Tremper's character.

Mount Tremper had a temper.

Now that Tremper sees his character, he is proud to be part of a small group of five. Who needs those "35ers"?

Mount Tremper
had a temper.

Then he learned a whole lot about
all the fun and interesting things that
make him special and give him character.

FUN FACTS

Of the five mountains in the Catskills with a fire tower on top, Mount Tremper has the lowest elevation. The other mountains are Hunter, Balsam Lake Mountain, Overlook, and Red Hill.

The Catskill Mountains have 35 "High Peaks," which are the mountains above 3500 feet in elevation at the summit.

Mount Tremper is in a small, teacup shaped valley surrounded by taller mountains. Off to its northeast, Overlook Mountain can be seen from its slightly higher vantage point.

The Catskill Mountain's hundred highest (there are actually 102 on the list due to a few ties) are the hundred tallest mountains in the Catskills. Tremper's fire-towered brother Red Hill takes the last spot in a three-way tie at 2980-feet.

Mount Tremper offers 2034 feet of elevation gain from its trailhead to its summit, which is the second-most elevation gain of the five Catskills fire towers (Hunter has the most). It also has more elevation gain than many of the Catskill 3500-foot mountains.

Mount Tremper has two lean-tos that you may camp at during your visit.

Be careful to watch out for snakes. It is possible to encounter a Timber Rattlesnake during your visit. It is important to stay calm and not bother these animals!

There are also black bears in the Catskills, and they are known to visit Tremper Mountain. If you would like to learn more about bear or snake safety, feel free to visit the NYS Department of Environmental Conservation or the NYC Department of Environmental Protection for more details.

Made in the USA
Middletown, DE
11 March 2023

26446417R00018